JUST AS I AM

Jenny Zellers

May 18, 1983

This book is a reminder that
your faith is all about life and
that in the midst of it all _____
God is with you.

Board of Christian Education
1st Congregational U.C.C.
St. Joseph, MI

JUST AS I AM

written by Jane Graver
designed by Kathy Counts

Concordia Publishing House
St. Louis

COVER—Photography By Brian Hendershot
Designed By Kathy Counts

Photo acknowledgments

Greer Cavagnaro/17, 41, 48
Bob Combs/8, 38, 47, 56—57
A. Devaney, Inc., N. Y. Robert Weichert/60
Shirley Heck/11, 42—43
Brian Hendershot/12, 23, 54
Harold M. Lambert/34—35
Robert Maust/65, 66
Religious News Service/77
Steve Richie/6—7, 24, 27, 37, 44, 59, 75
H. Armstrong Roberts/71
Blair Seitz/68
Fritz Schaeffer, Studio West/73, 78
Spectrum/14, 52
UNICEF Photo/33
Wallowitch/18, 20, 28—29, 30—31, 62
Brass Shutter/51

Concordia Publishing House, St. Louis, Missouri
Copyright © 1975 Concordia Publishing House
ISBN 0-570-03035-8

MANUFACTURED IN THE UNITED STATES OF AMERICA

10 11 12 13 14 15 16 17 18 19   1B   90 89 88 87 86 85 84 83 82 81

CONTENTS

a GOOD DaY

I'm going to clap my hands
snap my fingers
skip down the street, singing loudly
leap a few fences
ride on a swing till my feet touch the sky!
The neighbors will probably think I'm crazy,
but I'm so happy I just have to let it out!
No special reason.
The world just looks extra beautiful to me today
the sun feels extra warm on my back
all day long my mood was silly and giggly
people were laughing *with* me, not at me.
What fun we had!
I know You are the source of all joy.
When I express how I feel, I'm praising You.
Thank You for this good day.

Psalm 47

I don't know what got into me, God.
I'm so ashamed of myself I could die!
I'd like to crawl into a deep dark hole
and never ever come out.
How can I face them again?
After what happened
they must despise me.
And yet, even now You offer me forgiveness.
Because You love me
and suffered for me
this horrible thing I did can be washed away completely.
Lord, I claim that forgiveness now!
Not because I deserve it
but because of Your great mercy.
Strengthen me as I apologize
to those I've hurt.
Let me make it up to them.
Help me never to do such a thing again.

Psalm 51

ASHAMED

It's good to be alone.
Now I can let myself cry.
Choking back the tears was hard
when she said those horrible things to me.
I didn't take it lying down, Lord!
I told her a thing or two.
The things I said hurt—
and I was glad.
Glad that I could hurt my friend!
That's awful.
Now that I've cooled off,
I wish I hadn't.
Maybe she's sorry too.
Or maybe she's so angry she'll never forgive me
never be my friend again.
God, what should I do?
How can I mend this broken friendship?
Forgive us both
and help us forgive each other.

1 Corinthians 13:4-7

AFTER A FIGHT WITH A FRIEND

my body

I know You created my body
and it's good.
Holy, even.
But those kids at school make bodies seem dirty.
I don't know what to do when they talk that way.
Sometimes I find myself joining them
thinking as they do
making a dirty joke out of something that should be clean
      and beautiful.
Forgive me, God.
Fill my body with Your Spirit.

1 Corinthians 6:18-20

WHEN I FACED MY PROBLEM

I feel as if I'd been carrying a fifty-pound pack
climbing up a hill
panting
staggering
almost falling.
And now the weight is gone
and I am free!
All during the time I pretended my problem didn't exist
it kept getting worse
and worse
and worse.
Finally I faced it.
Brought it out in the open.
Admitted — out loud — that it really bothered me.
We talked it over.
It's not completely solved yet,
but I can handle it now.
Thank You, Lord!

Psalm 30:11-12

My team is the greatest bunch of players ever!
And I didn't do too bad myself.
For once, we did everything right:
nobody tried to be a star;
instead, we worked together
encouraging each other,
setting up plays for each other.
It was a close game, but WE WON!
What a terrific feeling!
WE WON!
Thank You, God.
Help me be glad for the other team next time we lose.

Romans 12:3-8

WE WON!

Lord, I wasn't even there.
Not as far as my friends (friends?) were concerned.
Lately, they leave me out completely.
Sometimes they talk about a late-night TV show
or a movie I didn't see
or a party I didn't attend.
What is there for me to say?
I don't like being left out
but I don't know what to do about it.
Help me to remember You understand how it feels
and You care.
And, maybe, next time . . .
could you help me think of something neat to say?

Matthew 5:3-9

when i feel left out

new friend

God, thank You for sending me this new friend.
You know how much I need friends
to go places with me
to laugh with me
to share my innermost thoughts and dreams.
Lead me to choose the right friends
ones who will bring out the best in me
ones who will accept me and love me just as I am —
as You do.
Bless my new friend . . .
my old friends too.
Help me be a true friend to them.

John 13:34-35

I did it!
I climbed the ropes almost to the top.
Gee, it was scary.
My hands hurt.
But, for the first time, I didn't give up!
Thank You, Lord, for giving me a good gym teacher
who made me try harder
and wouldn't let anyone laugh at me.
I know You were there
in my teacher
and in me.
That makes all the difference.
Thank You, Lord!

Matthew 7:7-11

success in gym class

JEALOUSY

Lord, I know it's wrong to be jealous of my friend,
but I am.
I get tired of saying
"Congratulations" or
"I'm glad for you."
I want to be the one who
always has something new to wear
or is picked to do something special by the teacher
or gets a super special birthday gift
or wins the game with a fantastic last-minute play.
When I feel jealous,
remind me of all the wonderful gifts You have given me,
especially the gift of Your Son.
Show me how to be so full of love
there is no room left for jealousy.

Ephesians 3:14-21

MOVING TO A NEW PLACE

I don't want to move, Lord,
away from all my friends
away from this dear and familiar place.
There's a cold, sick feeling in the pit of my stomach
when I think about the first day at a new school
Saturdays in a new neighborhood
Sunday mornings at a new church
the whole family struggling with new jobs, new doctors,
        new activities, new everything.
I just know I'm going to hate it!
Maybe Joshua felt that way too.
You had to remind him You would be with him
on his way to the Promised Land.
What You told Joshua applies to me too; I know that.
This new place we're going to
doesn't sound much like the Promised Land to me—
but with You beside me, I'll give it a try!

Joshua 1:1-9

Sometimes I wonder what the world will be like when I'm
       grown up.
It might be destroyed by pollution
or atomic war
or all the natural resources might be used up
or there might be so many people there's no room for anybody
or . . .
The newspapers are full of frightening predictions.
Yet I know You are all-powerful.
You created the earth
and said that it was good.
You created people
and You love us.
Although we misuse the earth You gave us,
You'll never forsake us!
"How majestic is Your name in all the earth!"

Psalm 8

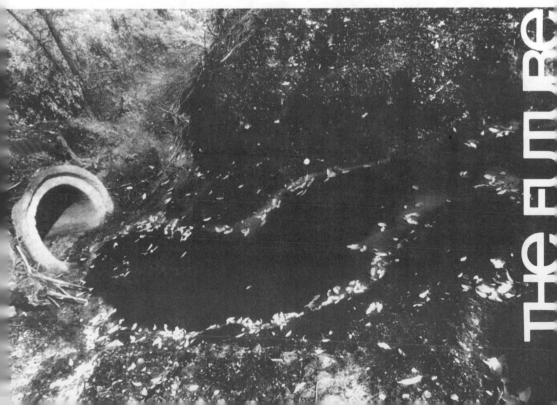

THE FUTURE

COMMUNION-
the first time

Today
I took Communion.
That means we're One,
You
and I.
Lord, it was different from what I expected.
I was so nervous
I really didn't feel like anything wonderful was happening.
But now I know
my feelings don't matter.
You *were* there
and You *are* here with me
right now —
very close to me,
loving me,
today and forever.

John 17:20-26

my new bike

It's so shiny
such a beautiful color
built for speed!
When I ride it I feel as if I'm flying.
Be with me as I ride my bike, Lord.
Help me take care of it.
Keep me safe.
Keep me considerate of pedestrians
generous to kids who don't have bikes
and always conscious that, like everything else I have,
the bike is an undeserved gift from You.
Thank You, God, for my beautiful new bike.

Matthew 6:19-21

Now I know what it is they've been whispering about:
a party—and I'm not invited!
It seems as if everyone but me is going.
Why was I left out?
Did I do something to make them mad at me?
Why don't they like me?
It hurts, Lord, to be left out like this.
I tell myself I don't care, but I do.
Thank You for being my true friend, God,
for loving me
for sticking by me
no matter what.
I know I am lovable
in Your sight.
Show me how to give and receive friendship.
Forgive me for the times when I've chosen friends for prestige
        and popularity.
Lead me to friends who share my true interests
and, even more important, my values.
Thank You, God, for Your comforting, steadfast, enduring
        friendship.

Psalm 142

NOT
INVITED

everyone LAUGHED AT ME

I messed it all up, Lord,
and everyone laughed at me.
Why can't I say what I mean without
getting my tongue all tangled up?
I know what I mean,
but it just doesn't come out that way.
I'm being very serious
and to other people I'm funny.
Help me to choose words well,
so people will take me seriously.
One more thing, Lord—
help me laugh at my own mistakes!

1 Corinthians 1:21—2:5

I wish I could go to sleep and never wake up
or run away and never come back
or step out of my skin and become a completely different person.
Anything to get away from this bad, bad day.
The hurts and disappointments of today replay themselves
over and over in my mind.
Right now I don't like *anybody*.
I don't even like myself.
There's a long list of things I should do
and I can't seem to decide which to do first
so I'm not doing anything.
Stupid, isn't it?
But I just read something even dumber—
in Your Book, of all places!
David feels just terrible.
Then he decides to sing!

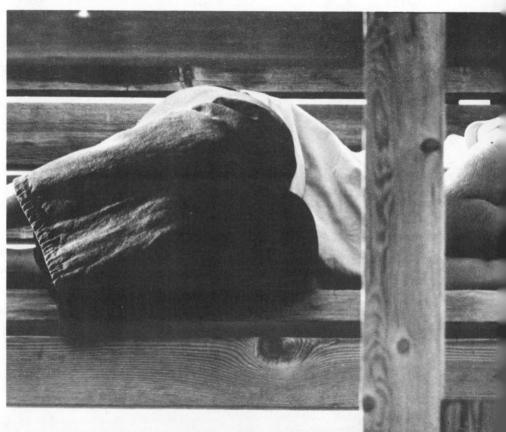

Sing?
At a time like that?
Ridiculous.
Unless . . . maybe . . .
the secret of claiming Your gift of a good mood
is to act as if I already have it.
I'll try it!
Thank You, Lord, for helping me change my mood.
I'm doing my part, see?
I'm smiling a fakey smile at myself in the mirror.
In a minute I'll find something interesting to do.
And pretty soon—maybe—I'll try to sing.
Help me!

Psalm 13

THankSGIVING DaY

"Lord, You have made so many things!
How wisely You made them all!
The earth is filled with Your creatures. . . .
All of them depend on You
to give them food when they need it."
Although we celebrate this day by eating a big dinner,
You've given me much more than food, Lord.
My clothes, for instance . . .
comfortable jeans, warm sweaters, bright shirts
my toys, books, games, sports equipment
the clean, warm, welcoming place where I live
my school, with all it means for my future
my family, all those people who love me
my friends
my church
my country
even my pets.
All the good things in my life are gifts from You.
My heart is filled with thanksgiving, God.
Forgive me for taking Your gifts for granted.
I will praise You
and rejoice in Your loving care.

Psalm 104, especially vv. 24-36

Every time I close my eyes I see that child.
Thin, sad face.
Big, hungry, hopeless eyes.
Crooked, skinny legs.
Swollen stomach.
How can You allow such things to happen, Lord?
What kind of a world is it when some people don't
        have enough to eat?
A sinful world, I guess.
A beautiful, fruitful world that men have spoiled.
Lord, show me a way to help children like the one
        in the picture.
I can't solve the world hunger problem by myself,
but I can do *something*.
Help me.

Matthew 25:31-40

PICTURE
OF
A
STARVING
CHILD

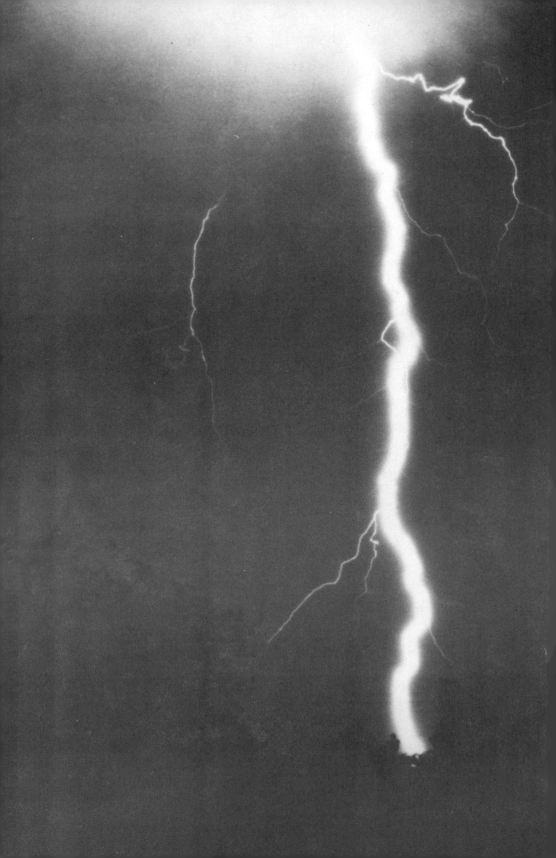

It's dumb to be afraid in a thunderstorm,
but I am.
If only it weren't so LOUD,
I think I could handle it better.
Now, if I had been in that boat with You and the disciples,
it would have been different.
Even though You were sleeping,
I would have snuggled right up next to You.
Then I wouldn't have been afraid.
But when I can't see and feel You close to me,
it's hard to remember You ARE there.
Next time I want to hide in a closet
I'll pretend I'm holding Your hand very tight.
With Your help
I'll act as if I'm not one bit afraid.
The disciples got over being afraid
and I will too.

Luke 8:22-25

afraid
in a
STORM

Is it wrong to spend a lot of time in front of a mirror?
I don't want to be conceited
but I really think
I'm better looking than I used to be.
I like that.
Thank you for the gift of whatever good looks I have
and keep reminding me good looks are not as important as
love
joy
peace
patience
kindness
goodness
faithfulness
humility
and self-control.
Help me to look for and value these things
in myself
and in others.

Galatians 5:22-26

MY TEACHER

I'm so mad I could burst.
Why couldn't she see how unfair she was?
Blaming me like that
when other people have done much worse
and she hasn't said a word.
I know it's not right, Lord, but at this moment I hate her.
Forgive me.
Come into my heart and turn my hatred into love.

Matthew 5:43-48

BEHIND IN MY SCHOOL WORK

I've gotten myself in a real mess, Lord.
Why did I let myself get so far behind?
It was really stupid
to put it off
and put it off
and I'm afraid now it's too late to catch up.

In his psalm David says You are gracious and merciful.
Does that mean You'll help me even though I don't
        deserve it?
I guess it does.
That's wonderful!
How will You help?
A miracle would be nice,
but I guess I'd better not count on that.
Will You help me
confess to my teacher?
accept the consequences?
work out a plan for doing the assignments?
organize my study time so I'll never get this far behind
        again?
I know You will.
It'll be hard
but, strengthened by Your steadfast love,
I'll do it!

Psalm 145, especially vv. 8-9

GOOD
REPORT CaRD

I'm proud of my report card.
I really did do my best work
most of the time.
But, to be honest, lots of other people worked just as hard
and didn't get grades like mine.
Thank You, Lord, for the gifts
that make schoolwork easy for me.
Lead me to use these gifts to serve You.
Lord, I know that kids who have trouble in school
are important to You, too.
You've given them other gifts
that make them special.
Help me look for the special talents
of each person I meet:
I want to see Your people through Your eyes.

1 Corinthians 12:4-11

failure in school

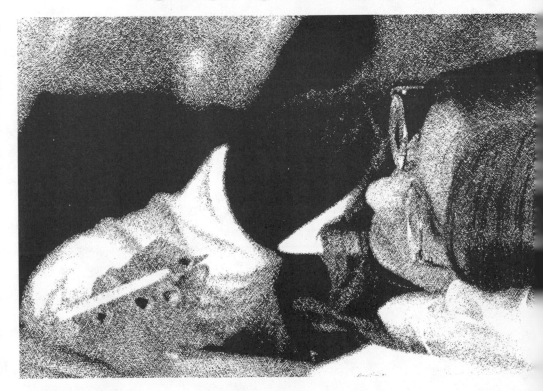

I failed again today, Lord:
failed to answer the question my teacher asked
failed to read aloud well—Lord, I stumbled over
        every other word!
failed to understand how to work those new math
        problems.
To be honest, I didn't even try.
What's the use of trying when I'm almost sure to fail?
Oh, God, I really don't think I'm as stupid as I seem
        to be in school.
When I'm away from there, I do okay.
But when the teacher calls on me,
I get so tense and nervous I can't think straight.
So I goof around and act silly,
hoping people will think I don't care.
Because You love me just as I am,
I can admit to You that I do care.
I care a lot.
Give me the strength to do something about my problem,
        Lord—and the wisdom to know *what* to do.
Show me how to get the extra help I need.
Bless my teachers and my parents; give them patience.
Bless me, too, Lord; give me self-discipline and
        determination.
When I feel surrounded by troubles, help me rejoice
        in Your love.

Romans 5:1-5

MY FAMILY

I look around the dinner table at the familiar faces I love
listen to the laughter, the teasing, the sharing
smell the good food Mom prepared
speak our table prayer.
Then I realized how very rich I am.
Like everybody, we have problems
not enough money
illness
bickering
hot disagreements.
But, Lord, You've given us love
love from You, beyond measuring
love for You, always growing
love that unites us to You and to each other.
Thank You for giving us the one thing we need most.

Proverbs 15:17

I'm so happy and excited I feel as if I might pop!
When I think of the Christmas tree
and all those presents under it
and the Christmas program
and the big family get-together
and no school for a week,
I get all quivery inside.
Thank You for the love and excitement that make Christmas so
 special.
But fill my heart and mind with the true meaning of Christmas.
You—a tiny, helpless baby!
Because You loved me, You were born in a place made for
 animals.
I don't want to be selfish and greedy like the innkeeper.
I want to rejoice in Your love
like the shepherds and angels.
Christ is born!
Glory to God in the highest!

Luke 2:1-20

CHRISTMAS
eve

THEY LIKE MY SISTER BEST

They like my sister best
and I don't blame them.
She's prettier
smarter
more graceful.
She knows just how to please them.
She gets the easiest jobs
the prettiest clothes
the most attention.
It isn't fair, Lord!
But when I point that out to her
she won't even admit it.
She claims I get the best of everything.
Could it be that she really means it?
That it's not just a trick to make me shut up?
That to her I'm the favorite one?
Lord, help me count my blessings without comparing to see
what You gave everybody else.
Free me from the bondage of jealousy.
Free me to walk by Your Spirit
in love.

Galatians 5:25-26

TEMPTATION

Lord, when You were my age did You want to
fool around in school
wander farther from home than You were allowed to go
talk back to Your mother
sneak off at chore time
join in with the others who pick on the kid nobody likes?
I guess You must have been tempted to do at least some of
        those things,
but You didn't give in.
I wish I could say the same about myself!
You know how hard it is to resist the pressure of the gang.
Did they call You "chicken" or "sissy" when You didn't go along?
Then You know how it hurts to be rejected
for trying to do the right thing.
Dear Lord, forgive me for giving in to temptation again.
Fill me with Your strength next time temptation comes.

Hebrews 4:14-16

when mom is sick

Is it my fault, Lord?
I know I haven't always treated her right.
I've disobeyed her
and talked back to her
and I've been inconsiderate, lots of times.
Forgive me! I'll try to do better—I really will!
Help me straighten out my thinking.
You don't punish people by making someone they love sick, do You?
And You do make good come out of bad things like illness and pain.
Please, Lord, if it is Your will,
make Mom well again.
We need her. We sure do need her.

John 9:1-7

Why me, Lord?
Why was I given this handicap?
Why couldn't I have a strong, beautiful, perfect body?
Because of this handicap,
there are so many things I can't do.
That's not exactly true, I guess:
can't isn't the right word.
But there *are* some activities that are hard for me
and some very close to impossible.
I appreciate that You've given me this handicap for my
          own good, Lord.
Your strength can work best through my weakness.
Through this hard struggle I'll accomplish more than I
          ever dreamed I could.
Frankly, Lord, I wish You had picked somebody else!
Oh, God, help me change my attitude.
Help me accept the things I cannot change.
Make me content with my weakness, for Your sake.
Fill me with Your power
Your strength
Your grace
Your serenity.

2 Corinthians 12:7-10

HANDICAPPED

MY BROTHER MAKES ME SO MAD!

Lord, why did You give me *him* for a brother?
I wish You had put him in somebody else's family.
He's always picking a fight with me
playing dirty tricks on me
messing up my things
teasing me
embarrassing me in front of my friends.
He makes me so MAD I COULD SPIT!
Lord, I know You don't want me to feel this way about my brother.
You love us both.
And You know that often I'm the one who's at fault.
Help me see him through Your eyes
appreciate his good qualities
and forgive his faults as You forgive mine.
Next time
help me see the joke when I'm being teased
show me how the situation looks from his point of view
give me the power to put aside selfishness and pride.
Lead me in Your way of love.
Bless my brother, Lord.
I love him.
I really do.

Matthew 7:1-5

NARROW ESCAPE

That was a close one, Lord!
For a few seconds it seemed as if death had come for me.
Even now I can't seem to stop trembling
when I think of what could have happened.
Even if I hadn't been killed,
I could have spent the rest of my life in a hospital.
Thank You, God!
Although I was careless, You saved me;
You protected Your helpless child.
No matter what the future holds
I won't be afraid.
You are with me
today
and always.

Psalm 116

They're moving away, Lord!
I might never see them again.
Even if we do get together next summer,
it won't be the same.
It helps — some — to remember that You understand.
You know what it's like to say good-bye to your friends.
You didn't do a lot of moaning about it, did You?
You talked mostly about seeing them again.
Help my friends and me look to the future as You did.
Be with them in their new home;
help them make new friends.
Be with me as I stay behind,
missing them.
Lord, thank You for the gift of friendship.
Thank You for being my best Friend.

John 14:1-3; 18-20; 27-31

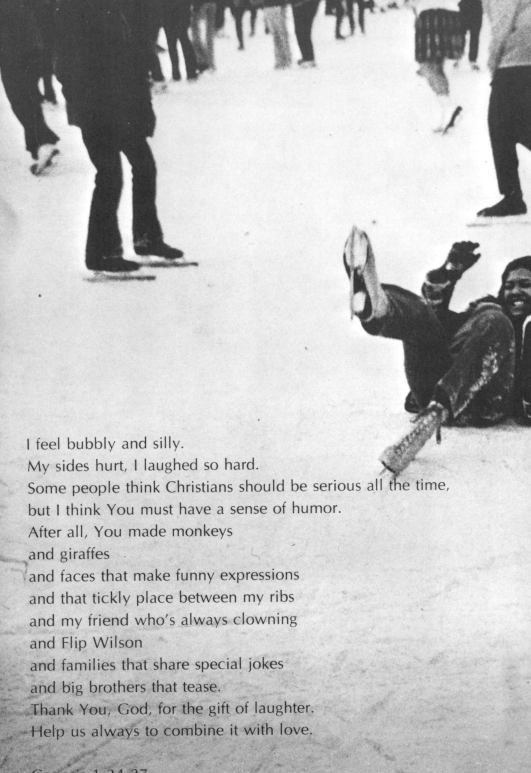

I feel bubbly and silly.
My sides hurt, I laughed so hard.
Some people think Christians should be serious all the time,
but I think You must have a sense of humor.
After all, You made monkeys
and giraffes
and faces that make funny expressions
and that tickly place between my ribs
and my friend who's always clowning
and Flip Wilson
and families that share special jokes
and big brothers that tease.
Thank You, God, for the gift of laughter.
Help us always to combine it with love.

Genesis 1:24-27

LAUGH-TER

too short

Oh, God, I get so tired of people making fun of me
because of my size.
Please, Lord, I want to grow
bigger
taller
heavier
stronger
and I want to start TODAY.
It's hard to always be the smallest one
the last one chosen for a team
the one the bullies pick on
the one everybody teases.
But then, You never promised that things would be easy for me
just because I belong to You.
God, make me big enough — inside —
to accept my physical size
to do my best with the body You have given me.
Still — forgive me, Lord —
I wish I were taller!

Philippians 4:10-13

He went to Heaven, they told me.
Lord, I don't think he was ready to go
      just yet.
We had too many plans
adventures we would have shared
a camping trip
baseball
building a giant model airplane
and now they'll never happen.
How could You let him die?
He's too young!
I feel angry
bitter
puzzled
afraid.
But "Let not your hearts be troubled,"
      You said, before You died.
You promised to prepare a place for my
      friend
and for me.
A very special place.
Maybe, after all, he doesn't mind giving
      up our camping trip.
Help me accept Your plan for my friend
and Your plan — whatever it may be — for me.

John 14:1-3

DEATH OF A FRIEND

easter
morning

I'm going to live forever.
That's really something, when you stop to think about it.
Almost unbelievable.
Like the events that took place on the first Easter morning.
A man died
and was buried
and wept over
and three days later
the angel said,
"He has risen!"
No wonder Thomas didn't believe it.
Nothing like that had ever happened before.
And because of what happened that morning
the fantastic
glorious
stupendous
gift of eternal life belongs to me!
We have good reason to sing our hearts out on this day!
Hallelujah!

Mark 16:1-8 and John 20:19-30

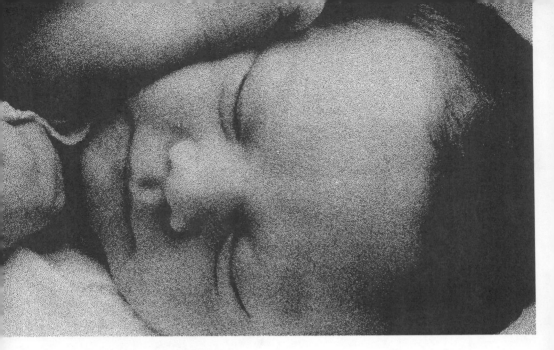

baby sister

She's so little, Lord,
so soft
so helpless.
I hold her in my arms
and she looks at me trustingly.
I give her my finger and she holds it tight.
She's the most beautiful baby in the whole world
and You gave her to our family!
Thank You, God!
Bless her, Lord, as You blessed those other children long ago.
Keep her safe in Your love.
Let me do my part in caring for her.
Keep me from feeling even a little bit jealous
of the time and attention she needs.
Help me be patient while I wait for her
to grow bigger and stronger so we can play.
Thank You, God, for my new baby sister.

Mark 10:13-16

My friend's father died.
I'm sorry for her
but even more, I'm afraid
because I know the same thing could happen to me.
What if someone I love dies?
Soon, I mean, instead of when they're old.
I couldn't handle that, Lord.
I just couldn't.
But Paul says You made death into a victory,
a very special happening
when a person becomes alive in a whole new way.
I guess when You decide the time has come
for my father — or someone else I love — to die and be
        truly alive in You,
I'll have to accept it.
God, I'll need a lot of help from You on that day.
My friend needs Your loving care now.
Be with her.
Strengthen her.
Use me to help her get through the days ahead.

1 Corinthians 15:35-38; 51-57

DEATH IN A FRIEND'S FAMILY

Today
I went on a trip to the strange and exotic land of Narnia.
Last week
I roamed the jungles of India
and explored the land behind the looking glass.
All in books, of course!
Books have given me so many interesting friends:
Henry Higgins
Misty, the wild pony
Tom Sawyer
Encyclopedia Brown
Elsa, the lioness
Laura Wilder.
Somehow it never occurred to me before
that the public library is also a gift from You.
God, You gave all those writers their imagination
their ability to weave words together to make a story.
Through them You've given me
learning
laughter
tears
suspense.
You've made me think about right and wrong.
And You guided people to put all those wonderful books together
in one very special place.
Thank You, Lord, for the public library.

Psalm 98

THE PUBLIC LIBRARY

DOUBTS ABOUT GOD

Are You listening, Lord?
My friend says You're not!
He says I'm silly and old-fashioned to believe in a God
who cares about me, personally.
After all, he says, think of the billions of people in the world
the many planets in our solar system
the thousands of solar systems in the universe
and the zillions of universes out there in mysterious space.
I've thought about it
and it's true, I can't explain
why You should care about a tiny speck like me.
But I KNOW You do
even though I'll never understand why
or how.
I know You care about my friend too.
Use me to help him.

Isaiah 55:6-13

SUNDAY MORNING

So that's why people go to church!
Up to now, I've always gone because I had to.
I'd sit there and look for ways to pass the time.
I'd make an airplane with the bulletin
or draw pictures
or count something weird like the number of German
        words in the hymnbook.
But today I really liked the hymns.
I even hummed a little under my breath.
And for some reason I listened to the sermon for a change.
I didn't understand all of it,
but that one part seemed to be written just for me.
All at once I felt very close to You.
I still do.
It's a great feeling!
Who knows? Next week maybe I'll even sing!

John 15:5-11

WHEN I FORGET
TO PRAY

Mom or Dad used to say my prayers with me at bedtime.
Now I'm big enough to pray by myself,
but lots of times I just don't do it.
Why do I keep forgetting something so important?
Why do I talk to You only when I'm in trouble?
Lord, please forgive me.
You were often tired, busy, distracted—
but time after time You went off by Yourself to pray.
Help me to be more like You.
I know You never forget me even though I sometimes forget
        You.
Thank You.
Show me ways to remind myself to pray.

Matthew 14:23
Mark 1:35; 14:32
Luke 5:16; 6:12; 9:28
John 17:1, 9, and 20

It really hurt You, didn't it?
It hurt a LOT.
I didn't know that.
Somehow I thought because You are God,
the nails and the thorns and the whip
wouldn't hurt You as much
as they would somebody like me.
You suffered all that because You love me!
It's too much to take in.
If You love me that much
I must be really special
in Your eyes.
Wow!

Romans 8:31-39

Although I've waited and waited for this day
now that it's here,
I don't feel one bit older.
Not until I remember myself a year or two ago.
God, You have helped me grow
in many ways.
I'm stronger
more even-tempered
more responsible
more self-confident.
You've been with me every day of my life
guiding me
protecting me
loving me.
The psalm says just what I feel today—
"Bless the Lord, O my soul!"

Psalm 103

MY BIRTHDAY

The whole day seems like a dream
now that I look back on it.
Yet there are moments that are still
          vividly real in my memory:
my nervousness just before the
          service began
my struggle for a steady voice as I
          repeated the promise
the pastor's hand firmly on my head
          for the blessing
the papery-skinned, fragile hands of
          the little old ladies as they
          shook mine, congratulating
          me
hugs from my family
gifts — especially that special one
the heady excitement of being the
          center of attention all day
          long.
Yet all these moments mean nothing
compared to what really happened!
Today I publicly promised to become
          a new person — Your person —
dead to sin but alive in You.
Give me the power to keep that
          promise
forever.

Romans 6:1-14

CONFIRMATION DAY

tomorrow

God, I just can't seem to go to sleep.
I keep thinking about tomorrow.
What if I make a fool of myself in front of all those people?
Even though we've practiced,
I might forget what I'm supposed to do
what I'm supposed to say.
I'll probably get all mixed up
and everyone will laugh at me.
And yet
I know You will be there to lead me,
You will be there to help me.
Remind me of all the times in the past
when, with You beside me, I have succeeded;
I've done well.
Even if I fail,
You've seen all the failures I've hidden from other people
and You still love me.
You'll be there, encouraging me
tomorrow.
Thank You.

Psalm 139:1-18

The more I study my country's history,
the more awed I am by the heritage you have given me.
Your powerful hand has given my country
natural resources
majestically beautiful mountains, rivers, prairies,
        forests, lakes
great leaders
citizens of many shades of color, many traditions,
        many talents
a government by and for the people
ideals of liberty and justice.
Please continue to bless our land, God.
Help us translate our ideals into action
to fight pollution
discrimination
poverty
corruption
war
instead of each other.
Keep us loyal to our country
but at the same time remind us
that our greatest loyalty belongs to You.
Help us always to know
the Lord almighty is with us!

Psalm 46

MY COUNTRY

Why do some people live in luxury while others are starving?
Why does peace among nations never last?
Why do even Christians fight among themselves?
Why do some people hate others because of skin color?
Why do You let people suffer with diseases like 'cancer?
Why are dishonest politicians not always punished?
Why do bullies get away with picking on those smaller and weaker
       than themselves?
I don't want to criticize the way You run the world, God,
but sometimes I wonder about these things
I do understand, a little bit:
You've allowed people to mess up Your beautiful world
because You want to be served by people, not puppets.
But even so, it doesn't seem right
that so much terror, hunger, and pain
should happen every day.
Lord, I trust in Your goodness.
In Your good time all things will be made right.
Even now, You understand the sufferings of Your people
and You grieve for them.
You can and do bring justice, mercy, comfort, and peace
to all who suffer.
I trust in Your goodness.

Matthew 5:3-11

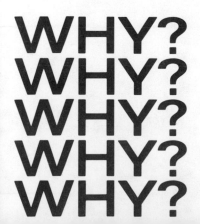